the book of sentences

UNIVERSITY OF CALGARY
Press

the book of sentences

rob mclennan

Brave & Brilliant Series
ISSN 2371-7238 (Print) ISSN 2371-7246 (Online)

University of Calgary Press
2500 University Drive NW
Calgary, Alberta
Canada T2N 1N4
press.ucalgary.ca

LIBRARY AND ARCHIVES CANADA CATALOGUING IN PUBLICATION

Title: The book of sentences / rob mclennan.
Names: McLennan, Rob, author
Series: Brave & brilliant series ; no. 45.
Description: Series statement: Brave & brilliant series, 2371-7238 ; no. 45
Identifiers: Canadiana (print) 20250223767 | Canadiana (ebook) 20250223783 | ISBN 9781773856476 (hardcover) | ISBN 9781773856483 (softcover) | ISBN 9781773856490 (PDF) | ISBN 9781773856506 (EPUB)
Subjects: LCGFT: Poetry.
Classification: LCC PS8575.L4586 B66 2025 | DDC C811/.54—dc23

The University of Calgary Press acknowledges the support of the Government of Alberta through the Alberta Media Fund for our publications. We acknowledge the financial support of the Government of Canada. We acknowledge the financial support of the Canada Council for the Arts for our publishing program.

Alberta Government   Canadä   Canada Council for the Arts   Conseil des Arts du Canada

The manufacturer's authorized representative in the EU for product safety is Mare Nostrum Group B.V., Mauritskade 21D, 1091 GC Amsterdam, The Netherlands. Email: gpsr@mare-nostrum.co.uk

Editing by Aritha van Herk and Helen Hajnoczky
Cover image: Colourbox 6862043 and 7051849
Cover design, page design, and typesetting by Melina Cusano

Everything arrives energetically, at first.

Mei-mei Berssenbrugge, *A Treatise on Stars*

When we name things simply, with words preceding
their meaning, a cosmic narration takes place.
does the discovery of origins remove their dust?
The horizon's shimmering slows down all other
perceptions. It reminds me of a childhood of emptiness
which seems to have taken me near the beginnings of
space and time.

Etel Adnan, *Shifting the Silence*

this sentence is from several failed attempts

Pattie McCarthy, *wifthing*

Table of contents:

BOOK OF MAGAZINE VERSE | 1

Four poems for *Parentheses* | 3
Three poems for *QWERTY* | 5
Four poems for my forty-ninth birthday | 7
Four poems for *Grain* | 9
Two poems for Emmanuel Hocquard | 11
Three poems for Poetry Pause | 12
Three poems for Broken Sleep Books | 13
Three poems for *Tiny Spoon* | 15
Three poems for *Poetry (Chicago)* | 16
Three poems for Kathleen Fraser | 18
Two poems for knife | fork | book | 19
Poem for *Train : a poetry journal* | 20
Four poems for *zarf* | 21
Four poems for *We Were So Small* | 22
Four poems for *Selcouth Station* | 23
Two poems for the Ottawa River | 24
Four poems for *Empty Mirror* | 25
Four poems for everyone I know who is currently dying | 27
Five poems for *The Paris Review* | 29
Five poems for Anstruther Press | 31
Four poems for my Patreon page | 33
Five poems for the moon landing | 34
Ten poems for Stephen Cain's fiftieth birthday | 36
Four poems for *Foundry* | 39
Four lines for Nelson Ball | 41
Ten lines for pagefiftyone | 42
Four poems for my fiftieth birthday | 43
Five poems for the Covid-19 global pandemic | 45
Five poems for *The Pi Review* | 47

THE BOOK OF SENTENCES | 49

Autobiography | 51
Two poems for RM Vaughan | 52
Three poems for *Lost Pilots* | 54
Four poems for my fifty-first birthday | 56
Autobiography | 58
Four poems for trees | 59
Autobiography | 61
Four poems for certain half-siblings | 63
Four poems for Joe Blades | 64
Four poems on receiving the AstraZeneca Covid-19 vaccine
    (first shot, | 66
Three poems for Heather Spears | 68
All I know about Tacoma, Washington | 70
Autobiography | 72
Mothers' Day | 73
Three poems for *Mouse Eggs* | 75
Three poems for *Scientific American* | 77
Quartet for an end of landscape, with farmhouse | 79
Lecture, on craft | 82
Four poems for Michael Dennis | 83
Song for a quiet voice | 85
Self-portrait, as preoccupation | 88
Autobiography | 89
Statement of intent | 92
The original photograph is more than a century old | 94
Coordinates | 95
Dream, with an interior | 97
Four poems for Ghost City Press | 99
I make my wife tea | 101
Seven poems on a return to the world | 103
Namesake | 106
Surviving, cottage | 108
Autobiography of green | 109
Quarantine, in perpetua | 111
Two lines for *Pocket Lint* | 112

The Alta Vista Improvements | 113
Burning the dead grass | 116
Four poems on receiving the Pfizer Covid-19 vaccine (second shot, | 118
Autobiography | 121
Summer, pandemic | 123
Sketchbook: | 126
Composition | 129
Rose and Aoife have eye appointments | 130
Composition | 132
Ars Persona | 133
The Garden | 135
As in Nowhere, No-One | 136
Approximation | 138
From an essay on Jean Valentine and Emily Dickinson by Julie Carr | 139
Heat wave | 141
Reading Kaveh Akbar's *Pilgrim Bell* by our new inflatable pool | 143
Composition | 147
Pastoral | 149
Autobiography | 151
Four poems for *Mary: A Journal of New Writing* | 153
Rose finally gets a fish | 155
Yesterday, not my photo | 158
My father rode in a helicopter | 160
Who I am today | 164
Rose collects a second fish, to replace the first one | 165
Autobiography | 168
Four poems for Douglas Barbour | 169
Four poems for Peter Van Toorn | 171
Autobiography of blue | 174
Six anti-ghazals for Phyllis Webb | 176
Rose finally gets a third fish, | 179
Acknowledgements: | 183

BOOK OF MAGAZINE VERSE

Four poems for *Parentheses*

1.

I shall begin with slush, and the bone cold prominence
of icy blacktop. To break this open,

is to understand the weather. Patterns, patters,
geographic upturn. An Alta Vista flock

of stopped, stalled cars.

Snowsuit, snowsuit, backpacks. Domestic chain.

This little wild, writing out
such bureaucratic document

across the school board: buses cancelled.
Trapped. A more
prosaic field. Having fallen from the sky,

remaining children skate haiku
over playground inclines: one line,
one line,

stop.

2.

Whereas this scene
was finally cut:

3.

I have aged here,
underneath the grey. A solution

of salty brine.
To see clearly now,

impossible. We roam by memory,
combined will,

and freezing rain. They sizzle
and dance. To gesture

is to know the features. Crossing guard,
she knows me,

safely beckons. Calm,
combining measures: silver,

sea stars. Her red
and tender gestures. Stop sign,

binding unplowed paths.

4.

To wonder: what might you know

of this from there, your Barcelonian tides?
The loops of language,

cadence,

cable, telephone wire. Where
does writing begin? Held

by hardened drifts, stone breath, this
three-winged plow. A name

between two limits.

Three poems for *QWERTY*

1.

I do not wish
to repeat myself. The Saint John River.

A tributary forms. A young woman
walks into a room.

A pencil mark

attends an edit. Wind chimes, windowsill,
a scarecrow. Small rise,

mountainous, you see. We place
a marble on the floor.

2.

I do not wish
to repeat myself. Bountiful, and good,
the shallows where

the people. Forms

a sentence, passage. Rolling hills,
hydronium, this

unrankled body, speech;

linguistically transmitted,
a breathless

oratory. Hush and paddle. Swim, the eddies
tarnished through affection.

3.

I do not wish
to repeat myself. An artifact
of river valleys. The chemistry

of restless forms. Is this
transition. I seek

the guided portrait. Homestead,
self-replicating. Decentred

mediums. Lawful, and

chaotic. Full moon, eclipse,
police thyself.

A fabrication

of fossil language. Saint-Jean,
Wolastoq,

unspoken hearth. A lone explorer
standing, at

the snowy edge.

Four poems for my forty-ninth birthday

1.

A seismic accumulation. Words as slow as paint.

This memory, pastoral. My father: a handrail,
new against the homestead,

his unsteady gait. A shoal
in his head.

If this a fixed point: I have felt this age
forever. Surroundings swirl, and shift.

2.

The O-Train as it snakes, construction. Timetables,
walked and walking. Wherewithal.

They aim to build this

needlessly slow. I kid, of course. But then:
the concrete

does nothing to absorb the water. Floodplain,
streets. The carved precision

of caged liquid. But,

the clouds. The lightest rail.

3.

Bang on: the texture of
an instant. Letters patent, by which

we mark such passing. Year
against idiot year. Simultaneous,

this miniature. How to defend
the little beasts of wear. Would rather

this than otherwise, long
in my death-bed.

4.

Disorienting: just how large is forty-nine?
What

are numbers, really? What is a year? I can't
wrap my head around, mid-

century clatter. Resist! Old enough
to have a daughter

who marks her milestones. The pages
flip, flip back. A wooded terrain

of pineapples, sage. A hand-
carved dream.

We are all born free

of history, until. I set my age
to airplane mode. Hold on.

Four poems for *Grain*

1.

Compression-fields. If I put so much time into writing. A grave
the size of a hand. The grass

will swallow anything.

This, your invisible counterpart.

2.

Fourth cousins, a century-plus
since their western expanse. A contrail. Something

for everyone, this contest
of quarter-squares.

Set ashore. Approximating
patience. Between Earl Grey

and Craven, a burial of MacLennans,
the separation

of a single vowel.

3.

To paraphrase John Newlove: In this cold room,
smeared

with human nature. A wintertime of zeal,
and homeschools, books, all dripping

from the sun. A season's facts,

in violation
of community standards.

4.

And for a while, the walk is productive.

Two poems for Emmanuel Hocquard

1.

As if it could be taught. Sedimentation, the ruins
of elegy, light. So lush. No words

but the imagination.

2.

Foot paths
confuse the wilderness. The wood:

a sentence, divided. Speak to me. A book

I might forever write. I am
alive, I am alive, I am

impossibly alive. I am most likely dead.

Three poems for Poetry Pause

1.

What else we carry

in our bones. Glass, grass, and
delicate presence. Rolling verse, translated;

sound

like living cells. Searchlights, garnered. Integrating
letters, numbers, roots of space.

This might be imagined. The surface
of a glass of wine.

2.

Each body

marks us. The entrance
to Pompeii, the needle's glance. There is nothing

to explain.

3.

The author

of this handmade tale. A stitch, across
a weathered sentence.

Like a flow of speech. A curious

seaside feeling.

Three poems for Broken Sleep Books

1.

How to retreat from a sentence. Clear panels, absent
a future. The quilt of empire.

This February, winter. Coats the yard. A blank page
so rarely empty.

Poetry: I don't know what that is.

Such patterns of storytelling: resolved
to reinforce myth.

2.

This might have been a mistake.
One plants a flag,

sets boundaries, storms the beaches.

Legion. I could get lost counting.

When the first peoples emerged, we know
so very little. Down from the mountains, trees,

the lake. A breach, at the bottom
of Grand Canyon.

To speak of hunger, laws. A full possession.

3.

All origins
are guttural. The body, like

the letter. Divides. Within the boundaries
of any given. Steal away. We want

what you want. Occasionally, silence.

Three poems for *Tiny Spoon*

1.

A string, tied   down to earth. February sun,
compared to music. In full view

of the nightly plow.

2.

To bury, nature. Sketch in a notebook. The altitude,
an accumulated thirty centimeters. Echoes,

blooms to black thread, white.

3.

An immortal

stillness, gathers. Somewhere, light is filtered. Somewhere,
a thin form, mostly paper, melts

beyond the snowy limbs.

Three poems for *Poetry (Chicago)*

1.

Circumvent the width of a small phrase, a
particular memory.

Sleeps, an empty house. My father, stoic. I begin
to copy out everything

that was said. Diagnostic adjustment. These
handmade books. It is hard to know

which words might be missing.

2.

A thermal invention. Rooted,
in particular speech

or calm. My mother, permanent
in upholstered corner. Her meteorological dispatch,

distributing shawls and sweaters across

a chasm of her
frigid surfaces. At their insistence, keep

the thermostat at par, static. Melts,
across the seasons.

3.

Her hospital years. I raise
a curled hand. My mother's radius

of remaining rooms. Dialysis, line
below the collar bone, scar-tissue

stretched

across the septic. An expectation
of broken glass, eggshell, blue-white

bedsheets. Wondering,
in what proportion

does it bleed.

Three poems for Kathleen Fraser

1.

If I were to pin all my favourite quotes
this wall might collapse.

2.

The elegy speaks to an absence
both unexpected

and abrupt. Applies
lyric pressure. *She speaks to me*

in sentences. Solitude

as capital. Echo, across
these crystalline structures. Poem

as carved diamond, or
a certain uneven

panic.

3.

The pleasures that conflict
from this writing. Loss

is a loss.

Two poems for knife | fork | book

1.

Poetry: a resistance, stocked. Within these walls,
enough to flood

Spadina's passage,

each nineteenth-century window. *Speak to me*
of the principled stance. And the conviction that wisdom

lies in books.

The Bellevue Estate of George Taylor Denison,
one hundred acres

of interjection: a low-rise marketplace
of patterned shops and grocery,

this brightly-coloured quilt.

André du Bouchet: I will repeat myself
like earth you tread.

2.

Gadding, smalls. This spare notebook leads
to highways, alleys, loops

of cellular, broadcast. Cold knowledge,

passion; a poem

might pronounce in shadow, lifts; the transparency
of disappeared. A stream of fluent,

bewildered power. Signaled.

Poem for *Train : a poetry journal*

Enough grain. Pointed west,
and fast enough

to lose all fear. I was on a train,

a compact meditation
of grammar,

grounded. My thirtieth year:

parenthetical towns and city-stops,
a break-line, gathers. Speed

enough to empty. Ontario spreads,
a night of long winds,

winded. I wish

to see the world,
they said. And sped

till morning. Third star
to the right.

Four poems for *zarf*

1.

If there is any reason to be dissatisfied.
I could hear the difference. The world began
with arms akimbo,

imagine. These parabolic

orbits.

2.

The fluid dynamics of a
small description.

3.

The roots of fear: if I ever made
such a conscious decision. A sentence,

and a sound of wheat.

4.

Nakedness of air, of sky. Will prolong
themselves in fragments. The permutations

are endless.

Four poems for *We Were So Small*

1.

I lay with whispers in the margins. The day
emits an undertone, a vocal break. This tree

has no branches.

2.

To leave a door unlocked; is all
temptation.

Seeds to start in February: artichokes, arugula,
asparagus, broad beans, claytonia,

corn salad,

mustard, onions, pac choi, peas,
radish, spinach.

3.

Compare each step into that river. This
untimely end. We navigate

the inevitable. But
the clouds.

4.

To say: I wrote these words.

Four poems for *Selcouth Station*

1.

To agree with my step. Language,
clouds. They float.

2.

Bobbypinned, echo. An imitation
of linked pages: trimmed. The same

is not different. It is the same.

3.

A migration of lyric, facts. This poem
an integral part

of a research-based process.

4.

One might introduce pressure. This converts
either to diamond

or fossil.

Two poems for the Ottawa River

1.

I live in a city built on story. The transparency
of our gathering. Meniscus: a poem, bound

by the ends.

2.

I live in a city. The water, fractured. Runnels weaken
fresh montage of sandbags, stone berm. This work-

in-progress. A mutilation

of language, sweat. What abnormal waves
curl; consume neighbourhoods, streets. Further

record-setting rain. Constellation

of tree-root, porch light, abandoned cars. A starry
misfire. Two metres high

and surge.

Four poems for *Empty Mirror*

1.

Language still takes time

to adapt. The colour of spring
balm, a tongue. The amplification

of syntax.

What have you.

2.

His hospital years: the median
of my father's temperament. A memorial

of day's events: *Mythbusters, Dr. K's
Exotic Animal ER*, or the Smithsonian Channel,
multiple documentaries on Hitler,

and World War I trains. His days reduce
to a single floor: this radius of twenty feet,

and wheelchair jaunt up the lane
to the mailbox.

3.

It follows
that one speaks: the curl

of good will, vanished

from origins. Lament. I like
this universe. What shines

is the appeal.

4.

Oh, humanity. The season finale
is upon us.

Four poems for everyone I know who is currently dying

1.

Enough, I'm forced to make a list. Three, possibly four,
across the past few days.

No detail of your body is safe. The house
is empty, spills. A pension

of false leads.

This poem's publication
will outlive you. And the ones who won't

survive to witness, this.

2.

I am on a postcard, headed north, seeking the source
of the cold. Where it withers,

backtracks, loses. Permafrost, bobby pinned, held

in imaginary place. Between thaw and extinction, entropic
stretch of horizon. One million

animal paths.

3.

Cancer, that bastard malignancy. *Idiopathic
Pulmonary Fibrosis*, a solid aggregate

of lung tissue, morphing to stone. *Amyotrophic
Lateral Sclerosis.* Anatomy

that consumes; turns in. Get your
affairs in order. So many

affairs. Two years, he says,
if he's lucky.

4.

I will cross that bridge
when I get there.

Five poems for *The Paris Review*

1.

Texture of an imitation of an imitation of her hairstyle. Here
the heart agrees

with my patter.

2.

The mud the children track through sunroom
more imagination

than memory. If composing poems are a kind
of translation. If editing is a kind

of translation. If hiring some kid
to mow the front lawn is a kind

of translation. Everything, perhaps, is translation.

3.

This darkness, mere light. The practice
of ancient, and everyday. Letter carrier tethers, our

boundary of lawn. Bluesky ethics: you can never step twice

into that same thread. Topography
of a thousand swoons.

4.

Hardtack, dusk. I drink

like a glass of wine. Because time is a river and the breeze
is a river and the

dandelions are a river. Collect in their small hands, two
modest piles pool

on concrete steps. For now, spring flows
in their direction of laughter,

attention. Bottleneck, stars. Our street today

, an implausible word.

5.

Unfastened, listen. They

break for the house.

Five poems for Anstruther Press

1.

Whether a lake in the Kawarthas,
or this Scottish coastal town

founded as fishing village. Stumbleweed,

euphemism. Alexander I of Scotland, and
the lands of Anstruther

to William de Candela,
1225. We all fall down. This sentence

is preposterous.

2.

Amid a network of freshwater lakes, this glacial stretch
of shining excess. Lake Ontario, via Anstruther Creek,

by way of rivers Mississaugua, Otonabee, Trent. A drop
of dew, line. Bhanu Kapil: *What*

is the place of the fragment in your work?

Picture the river. The water, flows. What
has been transferred. Names, we

carry. Here.

3.

A poem to the reader: territory, maps and dust.

Invasive species: as Stacey Ho writes of ecologies,
migration, refugees, metaphor. It has

me thinking.

4.

Anstruther: a name
that lends itself to water. One small boat fishing,

coasts alternating wavelengths: cyan,
turquoise, teal.

The Great Lakes basin. Billy the Kid and
the benefit of ash, oak. A strained relationship

to sun. Semiotic, tidal. Plants
a bare foot.

Preoccupied by gravity,
the surface water points to sea.

5.

Articulation, falls.

An unobstructed view.

Four poems for my Patreon page

1.

In the midst of long summer, one weathers the distance. Plastic pools, spools; occasional childcare. Begin to count minutes, down, from a passing car window. Red or blue ink, and the nature of memory. So much is complicated. Breadcrumbs, breadcrumbs, passage: what it means to record. Sidewalk, the sprinkler; mass of drawn paper. This day at the park. My two small daughters lay in the margins. They pick every flower. They criss-cross the paths. Their hands in my hands.

2.

There, in the sky, lay a stitch.

3.

The challenge for slackness: to breathe. Amid flurry of space, wounds, tasks: meal prep, dishes, laundry. The length of the sentence. The length of a paragraph, punctuated by naps.

4.

Sit, then. Keyboard position. See reverse for care.

Five poems for the moon landing

1.

In archival footage, Neil Armstrong steps forever
onto the windless surface

of humanity's first poem. His right boot pressed
more permanent than stone.

To paraphrase Spicer: Hold to a past
that saw this future

with firm hands.

2.

Twenty years to that day, my father monologued
the moon landing in our homestead kitchen

for five minutes, before I realized
he was speaking

to me. And then he went outside,
continuing his work day

unabated.

3.

That day he landed, fell
to earth. On Adam's Peak, a terran

counterpoint. The left foot
speculates.

4.

This half-century of origins: the eagle

has landed. Rocketman, Starman, whether
life exists on Mars.

Remember: on prime time,
a contemporary police detective

disappeared from his desk

to land at the end
of the Nixon era.

A speechless
crackling score.

5.

From lunar targets,

a search
for the good. My father

grounded, finally. A wheelchair path
through familial space.

Excuse me: a Major Tom
is here, sir. He has brought with him

a list of questions.

One giant leap
across a lesser gravity.

Ten poems for Stephen Cain's fiftieth birthday

1.

The endlessness of experimentation
across

this grey anchor
of urban agglomeration.

2.

In an absence of wholeness,
poems neighbourhood, gather,

quarter-centuried,

tethered. The subway
flickers past

an ambit of chicken wire,
garden.

3.

One listens, for patterns. Helped
you move, once. I

remember that.

4.

Perilous headwinds, crater.
Check default, bobby pinned;

this montage of Dundas West,
Keele. Riddle

me this: are all the words here
spelled correctly?

5.

The house at the end
of the end of an incline,

arteried. The community bedrock
rolls nightly.

6.

Paralexicon:
a body is made

by reversing a word
inside a word.

7.

Where

did your novel. A flooded closet
of small press. Here, a 1909 seam

that stitched the fabric

of original city
to West Toronto Junction.

A confluence
of Indigenous trails.

8.

A mannerism of made speech,
of which all language

is. Am reading: does
anything hold up?

9.

A decalogue, for fifty years.

Raymond Souster: "It will need
all of death
to take you from this corner."

Whether footprint
or footnote.

10.

Stand in the light. Where
I can see you.

Four poems for *Foundry*

1.

Choreographing a boundary

of seasons: held out and held, a chromatic portrait
of meteorological suspension. May freezing rain,

pellets, the savagery

of Ontario spring.

2.

Log, supplemental: an element
of ancient passage. It

snows.

3.

This vocabulary: poured,
as casting. A biography: rejected with spirit,

undermining the recesses

of eventual summer. Snow enough
and cold we beg

for rain.

4.

Finally, to say:

I was warmed by the sun.

Four lines for Nelson Ball

A word,

hush.

The word,

hush.

Ten lines for pagefiftyone

To be both simple,
yet confounding.

The ways in which this sky
adheres to rooftops.

The insect corpse-shell
gripped to summer's tree.

To set this all down
in an unrefined manner.

Nathanaël: The word
precedes the body.

Four poems for my fiftieth birthday

1.

In the details, bedeviled. Am I half-way finished, or begun? Too
    soon,
by half. A ladybird, floats. My bare hand. Homestead,

sunsets. If I did complain. Characters in snow and shadow,

ghosts of every childhood
that blossomed: my father's, my sister's, mine. Familiar sounds

so simple, they amplify. Echo.

2.

Since the beginning, when I found
my mouth, a mumble, let alone

a voice.

3.

From almost any angle. Busted a toe, and then a second.
These inaugural fractures, after nearly five unbroken decades

of carefree indifference. Almost every day,
I stood. I stood up. Imagination, bristles. I

remember, like it was. Margins, where
I lay this ancient peak.

4.

Memories
of a distant, faded thing.

Five poems for the Covid-19 global pandemic

1.

The curve of the inevitable, against
the unforgivable. This cancellation of birthdays, school boards,

government offices. A list of essential services, and declarations
of various states of emergency. Might

the highways close? Might

the blood boil? How we hunker to hand washing,
laundry, supplies; the open air

of Disney plus. Unsettled. A check-in with eldest daughter,
to see where they're at.

2.

A cough, amid the freezing rain. My health-compromised spouse
and ailing father, where

do we situate. Where do we begin.

3.

Social media feeds of barren store shelves. Empty streets, though
we don't leave the house. Slow, snow erodes, dust

threads together spring hush. To attempt for a walk, the girls
pocket gravel. The rare passers-by, holding

six distant feet: this expanse, so as not
to cause harm. From a distance. The door

is our boundary. An exodus of extroverts
and introverts, alike. Christine, as

the latter, relieved.

4.

The porcelain

pixelated masses. I'm sure there are those
already writing their *Love in the time*

of Covid-19. Too soon? How bad, to how long. Our preschooler
checks out my heart, informs: "This side

is cracked." She recommends rest, and prepares
the plastic syringe. The American President's lies overwhelm,

contradict, solidify into a mass. *In exile
for the sake of the realm*. Where

is this heading?

5.

Happy first day of spring. Oh,
what a year

this week has been.

Five poems for *The Pi Review*

1.

Hypothetical: the distance
a poem may travel. Margins spill, a flock

of miniature birds
or ants.

One speaks to the long journey
and the short flight, the position

of the sacred. How far
and at what pace.

To include everyone, one must leave behind
this entire world.

2.

One speaks of positives, options; a way
back home. A pandemic

of misspelled options.

Picture the lily. Filament, labyrinth, treacle. Vines
parry, jostle, pick apart

the bonds. A brick wall groans
against the pleasure

of a single seed.

3.

I can tell you
anything.

4.

When we say forever, we do not mean
without end. We have been here,

but at one point, we
were somewhere else. The limitations

of a single myth. I am airplane,

starling, patterned
clipper. The sedentary rudiments

of layered rubble.

5.

Picture the house. These hands
are spilling. Rise up, gather. A concordance

of flowers, stone, abandoned clothes, his
errant speculations. I am not

your noun, your verb, your
action word. It is

impossible to write. My father's texts

have reached their end.

THE BOOK OF SENTENCES

Autobiography

Listen: any two are opposite. The green
is cleaved. This infinite summer.

Lawnmowers. The children
mourn their loss of dandelions.

This busy street. Without which there might be
no poem. We gave these children

names; that we ourselves
had never held.

I realize I am far away. The power of the group chat
is the tether. I think on endings

and revise.

Remaining on the ground, with me. With them.
They gather sticks and weeds and bits

of string. I've been here long enough.
The point is not

to come away, unchanged.

Two poems for RM Vaughan
(1965-2020)

1.

Ten reasons why and why and where and back
in the days when your poems had the

longest titles, lists

of what could otherwise be im-
possible. Now, a list of news
you could not experience: how NASA

discovers evidence of water

on the sunlit surface of the moon; how
the stars might shine; the death

of Diane di Prima. I catch

the opening of her poem, "The Window":
"you are my bread / and the hairline

noise / of my bones / you are almost
the sea"

2.

I will not write you an obituary, it has been
but five days. It has been a week. It has been

the whole

of your life. Where are you? Now, they say
you're found, and now. A tribute

of dazzling, knitted scarves. Today,
the longest day. Richard,

we love you. Please get up.

Three poems for *Lost Pilots*

1.

This stateless, poetic. A succulent blue
rearrangement of shadows.

I seek out a headwind, the texture
of counterfeit; the ways

in which chemicals react. Overtasked,
overblown: this blue montage of sun.

I might see you, there. Lost pilot
in the stony ruin. Come fly with me.

Elevation of salt, of sand. The broad valley
empty

of any human settlement.

2.

Amid the semi-arid valley, an extensive
irrigation network. Faith, landscapes

the twitching leaves. A sidewalk.

3.

Dear heart, what group
of ill-fated pioneers

had travelled through this Great
Salt Lake Valley

in August 1846. Can
you see them, there. A trace.

A Sego lily. I ask: how
high up must you get. Is this

the right place. Drive on.

Four poems for my fifty-first birthday

1.

Unexpectedly, bare. A year into lockdown, pandemic,
an unexposed stretch. As a raw nerve,

housebound. The silence

of this great noise.

2.

Sawako Nakayasu: *Say Translation
Is Art.* Untended branches, shedding

burdensome leaves. The difficulty

of elegy, documentary, archive. The temptation
to speak, with hopes

of saying anything.

3.

The audience

ate it up. I can see

no connection.

4.

Parthenogenesis. We all scream
for ice cream. The long former vowel

of the English word "red": as
a reed.

Autobiography

To ascend, imagination. The condition
of a deep sleep.

Jean Valentine's pure blue country,
the way in which a sound

is balanced.

Four poems for trees

1.

Across this formal pleasure,
horizon contours mountain range:

sawmill, birdsong, lodgepole. Spilled

into my voice. Declarations of heartfelt territory

lost among these splintered branches.

2.

Frank O'Hara's subway,
and his blade of grass.

3.

Transplanting monkey puzzle. Prolonged,
a coastline errant. Ponderosa. Sechelt, breeze.

This sentence of foliage
reflects our complexities: such clear

and exposed. Abstraction, stripped excess
of tree-stubble. What season

of nouns. Audre Lorde: There is

no separate survival.

4.

Where my limbs meet yours, a poem
as dense

as a brick.

Autobiography

Cataracts are not grammatically correct. We took the surgeon's
     rewrites
into Stittsville, up the valley. Pembroke, shores. My vistas

mosaics of the dead and half-remembered.

To say: I could not see. A blur, of too much light; the light was
     brown.

Rosmarie Waldrop: The flesh of a bird.

Surgeon, cool gel coats my eye. The order of sleep and the occasion
of the bright light. Creates a hole in space.

The facts of walking, talking. Should have brought a book.

This is an oversimplification. Preoccupations, bargain. What I
     could
not find in the dark.

With two hands: mature cataracts, filtered perceptions

amplified. Heart rate challenged every sentence written.
The nurse, a headscarf tartan, Clan MacLeod. How did you know?

The blood will bring forth flowers, stately in-fills. It carried

the motion. My surgeon's edits, a break in linearity. Temperament.
Post-op

cookie, juice. Further cookies for the road.
My usual fumbling way. The circulation system

of a streetscape I can see. Highway 17

does not believe in eloquence. Little chapters. A roadside Noah's
   Ark.

We kept on driving. There were other bearings that required us.

Four poems for certain half-siblings

1.

Stylized: an American
metaphor. This Ottawa Valley lyric. Montana sunrise; where the
 sun

no longer rests.

2.

This gathering of halves: three states, two cities

in a single province. Point
of light. What else

may he have wrought.

3.

Inherited: these long, impossible eyebrows.
How the two elder trim, two

younger, less. At the center, I allow
the wild.

4.

If this is but half, one might ask:
which?

Four poems for Joe Blades
(1961–2020)

1.

Haligonian dervish, casemate. Hammond organ smooth,
you'd paint with envelopes,

couplets. A paper chase; a glue stick, scissors.
Compartmentalized

against a purity
of collage.

2.

Simultaneously, you wrote: no longer fit
for public consumption. An archive, heat.

Lord Beaverbrook. Puts down his foot.
Edwardian, Georgian. Elizabethan.

Radio, ratio. Across the airwaves. Where
the blues in the barracks,

sits. Aw, shucks. There
he goes, again.

3.

Four weeks following the death

of your father. Joseph Wendell Blades,
son of Wendell Blades. Flows

like ocean, waves. The Saint

John River. All
we might have known.

4.

Subsumed, by the time we'd heard,

all the way to ash. An archive, stacked.
And stood,

in shuttered storage. A bookmark; envelope
of scraps and salvage.

Of where you are,

and were.

Four poems on receiving the AstraZeneca Covid-19 vaccine (first shot,

1.

This unfamiliar pharmacy: lone strip mall beside row housing,
and the apartment where my grandmother lived

once she sold the house, and later, as

the doctor finally took away
her car keys. How long was she there? Before

her final weeks, resisting relocation

into a nursing home, arriving many years
beyond when she probably should. The silence

of low traffic,
plentiful birds. I park within an empty lot

and wait.

2.

I held   my jab, this
one good thing. An appointment, five days prior

to my high-risk spouse.

An epiphany, to profess. There was no pain,
no soreness, stiffness. A low exhaustion

impossible to distinguish

from this day-to-day. I mean,
pandemic.

3.

Ontario, a question   far closer
to silence

than monologue, dialogue. This blustering
of swagger, house rules, bubbles, the figure

of the body: how
has it evolved? We do not speak of blood clots,

bleeds. I reserve my anger

for what truly deserves. Our inept
premier, poorly preening

to pretend, before
he simply hides. I ask, again: how

has it evolved?

4.

A strip mall, five shops wide: the pharmacy,
within. Where, for a long time, two lots held

by Dairy Queens. Earlier still, two
Mac's Convenience. How

would one choose? Competition, clearly,

is fierce in these parts. Across Albion Road North, the empty
baseball diamond, sketched

in green. Awaiting players, this absence of crowds,

of neighbourhood children. How diamonds
are forever.

Three poems for Heather Spears
(1934–2021)

1.

Between fluidity,
attentive cells, an illustrated

pantomime. She captured medical standards, poetry
readings, courtroom action. The face

of stillbirth. Bedside

vigils. Hand, hand,
fingers,

thumb. A blueprint for intimacy,
against a vast

seduced indifference.

2.

Such papery fields: the animation
of a poetry panel, gestures

behind the open window. This filament of lines
our only access. An elusive quality,

from which there is only memory.

3.

My mis-pronounce of Van Gogh, responding
with her pulsing *Khokh*, hard-pressed

the guttural Dutch. She rolled
her eyes. She

savoured, stared. She handed
me my portrait. Here.

All I know about Tacoma, Washington
for my half-sister, who lives there

1.

Birthplace of Richard Gary Brautigan.
His hippy-blend

of early Hemingway simplicity, a stream trout
flung

into a parking lot, this city of destiny
on a Tacoma hill.

2.

My Montana-born half-siblings: a brother
in Sacramento, and she

in Tacoma. Our common biology: their father,
who does not know

that I exist. His choices
clear enough. Of which

we shall not speak.

3.

Show map of Tacoma.
Show map of Washington State.
Show map of the United States.
Show map of North America.
Show all.

4.

In order to understand: we consult maps,
by which to make a dialogue

more nuanced, held
in place. The gesture of a

gap.

5.

Richard, son of Ben Brautigan Jr., who had not been told
he had a son at all, until. Half-sister, now

I've known six months; dear,

and dear. Her sweet anxiety, sincerity. Five children,
some of whom are grown. Every Zoom call knits,

both balance, ground. An ether we have yet
to pierce.

Mayonnaise.

Autobiography

Neither a short talk nor a short walk. Once upon a time.

This poem might take one hundred years.

The plain language of the earth. Our youngest monologues
the long grass, anticipating mowers. In lockdown, the world

is through this window.

A period, begins. This point of exclamation.

I said, come out. To help determine rhythm. A jogger, passes.

To the subject of the phrase. Did Heisenberg complement each
      morning
with a dab of milk or cream, or neither? Tea or coffee? This blend

of molecules and dust. I take my coffee, black.

Outside, slippers hold grammatical function. Gain a perfect edge.
With minimal cars, a sweeter music. The syntactic ambiguity of

the madman in the yard.

I let the line breaks, break. A hesitation, fragments.

Morning meditations on poetics. Our panorama of apple
      blossoms,
cherry-coloured. Soon they'll stain the windshield.

No wonder I can't sleep.

Mothers' Day

1.

A space we leave for mothers. Ancillary: the possibility
of reading.

To slip into the next stage.

2.

Happenstance: this treatise on mothers: original, former
mother-in-law, ex-wife, current mother-in-law, birth mother, my

dear wife. A tension of the
short line.

When I was a little boy.

To maintain sequence. To live preoccupied
by such sentence. The ghost

of former selves, each layer another
habit of thought. Predates years. A grid of

vertical strips.

3.

I let the line breaks do the work
of punctuation. A hand-drawn card. I made her, once,

a bowl. The heart, at dusk. My mother is dead. My
mother is alive. Disaster

is a special case. A symptom. I am not your
period of relevance.

4.

If one could   provide some distance,
scatter.

Three poems for *Mouse Eggs*

1.

This hand-drawn air of musty typescript
on the actual page. Never trust a poem.

Artie and his beautiful chemical:
the Gold standard

of joyous, bittersweet. It is hard to live,
at times. Along Sainte-Catherine Street,

what marginalia

on the edge of the snow. I sometime think
I might chase

nostalgia forever.

2.

I'm afraid that I don't know. Dust,
the kind

that suffocates.

3.

This lightning of the possible: mimeo,
hand-stapled. A source

of real words, craft

and inarticulate softscape.
A roar, of eggs. How many must you

break?

Three poems for *Scientific American*

1.

A port of hosted ignorance. Faith or competence,
our curiosity

is wearing thin. The known knowns, and
the known unknowns. Disasters predicted, predictable,

and utterly avoidable.

The landscape of the left hand. Banjos plink
across the swamp. You hear it? Australia

burns, the Amazon rain forest. Begin with joy,
and end in failure. Joe Friday: just

the facts. How to seek protection; how
to push the world to champion

nature's green resilience? Dear Kermit:
sing. Your hungry cells

will saturate with sunlight.

2.

This mirror will not break. I've tried.

To go back to the beginning. Which?
A disagreement

of locution. Sad sack base, a pipe dream of utopia
or today's hot take.

Major Tom: unchanged, adrift. His body frozen, reflecting
light

from deep space, until that time

he might just pass a star too close. The quick embrace
of gravity.

3.

These inescapable facts: how science reveals. Don't talk to me
of alternates, denial. Rage. The economics

of the unnamed middle. Bush fires, quicken. The air
heats up. I

can't. My language
has abandoned me.

Quartet for an end of landscape, with farmhouse

1.

At first it was his stretch of fields, a lease
for a neighbour's expanding yield

once health forced him to pause. The spring
my father couldn't plant, Ontario sky

of variable spelling, monochrome, exaggeration
of slow cloud. His sleep apnea, diabetes plus

, that set retirement to root. Downstream, we watched three
tractors pull their crop of soybean

acres-clean across a morning.

A few years later it the land: shorn off and sold. This basecamp
of retained, remaining homestead: farmhouse, sheds, the barn.
   His cancer surgery

surpassing marks, a marked and marker. Held
his ground. A land   condensed. He drove

his gator to survey the boundaries. Where
he could not walk.

As ALS crept further, strolled electric wheelchair up the laneway,
hand curled up, around

the dog's leash, bounding forth.

2.

A farmer with no sons but one, who chose
a separate path. Embroidery of a curve

away. A daughter: thus, invisible. These
tiny changes made to earth.

3.

The nagging suspicion   of a counter of exchange,
an erased fenceline he could trace

ungrammatical. A birdsong, custom purposed   to
a steady, measured stitch of rain. A phantom

set of tree limbs, trails.   To watch him grasp

the cypher, signal, of each leaf, yet occupy
such bounds of silence. An unending pair

of ambit, errant children. A moment, as if
to stumble, still.

4.

My father, long and overcast.

Upon his death, pandemic: house is slowly emptied, harvest; strata
of a life well-lived. Disassembled, scattered; donations

and inheritance alike. Is newly occupied

through rental agreements, the shake
of one good hand. Eight decades of tenure, my father's
cremated remains;

        boy, am I

as hand-drawn figures in the landscape. Offered up as ghosts,
before the sun-bleach of the spring. These

blueprint pencils fade.

Lecture, on craft

Brightly-coloured painted, hand-drawn portraits, taped
to walls. A hallway marked, montage. Two sisters crayon-stand

stick-figured in the yard, or smiling stand with me, their
mother, a starry

sun. They sketch their late grandfather,
twig-legged, scissored.   Survival is not

an equivalent to wealth, a habit of thought. It is
survival.

Jean Valentine: I found this leaf / on my way to the post office.

Each pandemic-era loss. A standing list
of these remembered dead. Implied, what hope abides.

Not   the first death.
The ways in which   we
           swallow form. A crease

of each turned page.

Grief is neither infinite nor   unique. One asks
to sit a while with it, and

press on. A sometimes flood, an
impasse.

It is not necessary to acquire more   than you can carry.

Four poems for Michael Dennis
(1956–2020)

1.

A blue fade: tarantula arms
across Yasunari Kawabata's

sleeping beauties, petals; these
diminished leaves, another

white wall, poem. Where you sketched
Wayne Gretzky; lifting out, and up

his latest record-breaking win.

2.

Canvas on hardwood; two bare feet,
a claw-tub bathroom and

expansive bookshelves. A period
of morning, mourning

across every battle, the nature
of desire.

3.

The rain, you
wrote, it fell

like rain.

4.

What day of the week did you write
your poem about spiders? Where

did light fall, and in which
direction? I imagine

you by third-storey window,
facing Bank Street, possibly

nineteen eighty-six, or eighty-five,
cascade of businesses long emptied

along the Somerset to Laurier corridor,
dust clouds tunnelling the absolute.

Song for a quiet voice

1.

My great-grandparents' Mason & Risch upright acoustic, transported
via my father's pick-up truck

from Bank Street south to homestead circa 1976, and from homestead,
via professional piano movers

through pandemic's second spring. Along our Alta Vista shoreline,
this weighty asthma-trigger sets new anchor

underneath a lamp-lit moon. Some thirty years untouched, untuned,

the scratched, struck keys intermittently stripped,

and lining hammer, strings: the fossilized hulls
of sunflower seeds. The last remaining evidence

of an ancient clan of fieldmice, sequestered
in the farmhouse porch, a sanctuary

from housecats, loose snout of curious dog. My father's
routine passage. Immutable: the shelter

of underutilized behemoth.

2.

Synchronous to World War I, my grandmother's parents
purchased, thereabouts. Their Kemptville stronghold, whether

before he marked as Private, or beyond. Their two small
    daughters,
lessons. Returning, afterwards,

from Shorncliffe, mustard gas a cough that hung beyond

his weary lungs. It was all the suffering
he could do.

3.

Because they are machines, pianos
depreciate in value. Horizon-high

and happy tension. Through small hands the fallboard lifts
a confidence, as

our wee girls seek, explore the clarity

of nuance, pounding keys. They make up songs,
and broadcast, loud and jangly. Extricating dust-clouds

from dead cells settled there

from long departed kin: late uncles, aunts. Grandparents, and
their siblings. Informal gatherings of songs both popular

and spiritual, a non-
alcoholic brine served up in pots.

4.

An indeterminate rhythm. I plink out off-key attempts
at Satie, Nyman. The musty smell that permeates

the lid. Thirty-two years

is a considerable wait: these fingers recollect, but stumble.
Inherited: this brand of silence. What

my childhood self presumed that every household

held, until I pre-teen at a friend's house when I asked his parents,
sincerely, where theirs sat. My own years

of endurance: thirteen years of weekly lessons. Mrs. Williamson,
her sainted patience

and good humour. I did not want to be there. My mother and I,

unchanged, unmoved. At loggerheads. Each exterior thing. She
        wanted me
in lessons. Rosmarie Waldrop: the period

often does not mark the end   of a sentence, but a
        pause.

Self-portrait, as preoccupation

The period, how it missed
its mark. Unpunctured, punctuated,

standard in my later pause. It goes
unremarked. This

very small, and marked in
different, one might

say.

Autobiography

Plinths and ornaments; a cavalcade of bookshelves.

The pulsing energy   of continuity: e-learning
    mornings.
Rose, in headphones: jumping jacks. She smacks

a stack of paper loose, to the hardwood. A handful
of pencils, scraps. Their grade two

calisthenics routine. They shake
their sillies out. Across the living room, Aoife shifts and re-shifts

Zoom backgrounds: outer space, blue cloudscape, a temperament
of snow. She responds, when challenged: *My teacher taught me.*

Junior kindergarten sight words, reading: *the, a, she.* A writing
    grid
of nine, for Bingo, before they launch into a story

of a springtime frog. The blank space

of theoretical clarity.

2.

Home, home. We are home. We are endlessly, truly
home. Isolating daily rounds of paired coffee, corner office
　　margins.

Scoped and paired, these opposites rarely meet. Two positives
consistently orbiting the nuclei

of assembled, concentrated parenting. Alternating as lifeguards
for their e-school sessions,

a lineage of comparable sentences. The cat transfixed at
　　window-ledge,
abutting couch; preoccupied

with birdfeeder activity: black squirrels, a lone
red cardinal. He chirps the length of his curled tail.

3.

Each morning　　　　　　leaves its mark. The daily
　　accommodation
of dining room,

living room, kitchen. The news

is not outside; it echoes. They live out isolation, routines
set down by safety, science. School-released by mid-afternoon,

our wee girls scatter,

escalate their bedroom, backyard, basement. Swings and
climbing apparatus. Tablet videos

viewed from underneath their sheets. Our boundary

of suburban bubble. As streamed music blooms,

Christine flicks past
CBC hourly updates, lest the listening ears

of our small sponges, soak. Their questions, percolate. Will
you die of Covid? Will we? Why did those people get shot? We

answer shorthand, truthfully. We monitor, observe.
Attend. The

durability of the pause.

Statement of intent

1.

To cite the labyrinth, asking: where the poem takes you. The lawn
is not a habit. Odd details of human geometry. The routine

should not become constraint. A field

of possible action. Reflection had little
to do with anything. Abatement. This

is the hill I will die on. I live here. The land

upon which.

2.

At one point, Ovid   spoke to the crowd. He

digressed. At one point
in his exile.   Under construction, our street

has a different texture.

3.

Such pressure, printed. Exaggerated characteristics
and a lyric, lines that claim attention, digress. To be

more clever than song lyrics,   hold
the pulsing dance-beat.

4.

Beneath the weather, where we all are. Under. I hold
like a habit. Sound,

and then sense. Today,   my poem moved an
      inch,
and would not move again.

The original photograph is more than a century old

1.

The silver of multiplication. An umbrella. The rain draws, down
    the length
of the page.

To be unable to distinguish gravity from wind, or the familiar
    scent of wet sand.

Everyone in this picture is dead. Even the children. Even the trees.

2.

How something small might be recorded, whether general or
    specific.

You can prove to me the sun, the moon. The deepest rivers.

She holds the umbrella with her right hand. With her left hand.

If this photograph is reversed. We have no way to tell. The air
    draws colour.

In which direction the birds. In which direction spring. In which
    direction
form, or fire.

3.

In the beginning, was the rain. The silver, of manipulation.

The capacity for moisture. It rolls from the path.

Coordinates

1.

A shovel strikes pavement. Christine yanks a prominent weed,
only afterward realizing the triptych of leaves

that could immediately infect, spread an itch up each arm. The
    clusters
of interlude, possibility. Hard facts

and gristle. She showers   immediately.

2.

What else the wind gathers,   lone hedge
that separates properties, a northern border

parallel to our driveway. Cache of generations of foliage, scraps

of paper recycling, a plastic coffee cup, littered. Simply
the fact of a body: a puff of smoke. The

metaphor of the book.

3.

Mrs. Dalloway says she always purchased the flowers

herself. A consequence   trapped in a frame.
Christine steps

from the shower, the figure   of rainwater.
Our young girls

chaos around her, the economy
of green grass, laughter   , mismatched clothes.

4.

Each morning a collision of   sound
and disarray, sidelong

to each printed word. A painted design

of sunlight, steadfast traffic. Yawn of static,
the shadow perennials, our two daughters

set in the backyard, swings. Pre-dawn, quickly dressed
, they prepare

their own breakfast. Upon rising, I
bend toward coffee   , retrieve dustpan, broom.

Dream, with an interior

1.

Dream, with a tool. If this is rock, or stone. The stone
becomes hammer.

Rare outings mouth the words. We sing, behind the scaffolding
of facemasks.

I daily walk a slim incline, and steady. The ponderous framework.

A composite of inactivity, and lockdown patterns.

Robert Kroetsch: What is a letter? Sometimes it is a star that fell.

If dismember is the opposite   of remember.

2.

To translate, sound. Rose: the doorbell. Electronic adaptation
of Westminster chimes.

I can barely hear.   They saw the decades go,
    between us.

Toys on the shelf. Two towels decorate their floor.

I have been thinking, lately, of Falstaff. Let him come, they say.

Aoife: I am sad for your father. I remember Grampy. A name
they never called him.

To make so fine a point: in this economy?

To kneecap grief. What might that look like.

3.

An event, of saltwater. Rubble. Dreams of flying, falling.

And then,   she woke. Our bedroom doorknob,
   rustles.

Four poems for Ghost City Press

1.

To walk through water. The semantic slidings
of this guarded terrain. What is a city? The sky

is darkening.

2.

Abandoned measures: among the French, Haudenosaunee Dutch
and English, a Jesuit speech

ripples leaves across the sugar maple, the little leaf linden,
the swamp white oak. A speech

not dense enough to furrow, follow. Too orchestral
to hide behind.

The homestead elm. This salty brine. Ste. Marie de Gannentaha.

3.

A monument, a model. As any reader
might stretch across

the plain language of discourse. A speech-map

of the Hudson Valley. A tiny surface
interrupts. This long, hot

Syracuse summer.

4.

Mingling together. The salt
and the fresh.

I make my wife tea

The amenity of dailyness. Christine folds the last of our daughters
to bed, the curls

of their bedroom door, and a fresh

laundry deposit. As each of them birthed, Christine's preeclamptic
pressure,

a life threatening

montage,   discounting the possibility
of further babies,

and the space in the hold. Her IV drip, blood pressure monitor,

weekly medical checks. And where we might even put
a further human in here, every room

but the kitchen

belongs to the cat. A history
of unfinished thoughts, of stretched-out conditions. One
    perception

immediately follows. Upon landing downstairs, she pours her first
    cup
and abides. This forest of English: if our words

not exactly precise, we

approximate. Twining's Lady Grey, named for Lady Mary
    Elizabeth,
wife of Charles Grey, 2nd Earl. This black tea, with lemon

and orange peel, hot. The end, the end. The unobstructed
view. Such panoramic

can sometimes seem too immediate.

Seven poems on a return to the world

1.

To live is neither vertical nor horizontal. To ripple, outward.
Outward, in.

This stretch of fourteen, sixteen months.

I could imagine my body a map. Beyond imagination,
comparison.

A nesting of dolls. If you will. Of the fact of this writing.

2.

[

]

3.

Exclusions. Suddenly, a sense of rhythm.

This puff of smoke. We count trees. Request their names.

We demarcate dead relatives. The names of wildflowers.

Upon reflection: the only access to the infinite.

4.

[

]

5.

Hide in the bushes. Someone walks past. To re-learn conversation,
    speech.

Grammatical patterns, in soil. The point of a finger.

The way of apprehending anything. An element of structure.
    Someone

wants a baby to hold. We haven't any.

We listen for the bees; avoid wasps. Scan exteriors for vespiaries.

6.

[

]

7.

We survey mosaics. Underneath the groundswell, flowerbeds; the
pavement.

Another radius of blocks. A hesitation to emerge. Scathed, in the
essence.

This might be an elegy. An elegy to what.

Namesake

1.

The consternation, of multiples. Every figure is unique,
and with uniqueness, gathers. It is

your turn

to blink. A song of wetlands, shores; unravels. Where
are you going, and where

have you been? It will take more
than an anecdote, a pebble, scored forth

against a body, torn for clues.

2.

Many years ago: we walked, simultaneously, through
the commercial fields

of the world's largest airports. Unaware, adrift, this
is the impossible detail

of multiple languages   , of the entire text.

3.

How present is this narrative? How worn?
This

is neither English. An unheard thing.

Then, from this material. To hear them speak it.

Remembering those weeks I nearly blind.

Remembering that time   I wrote a poem.

Surviving, cottage

1.

The risk, at which we read   the senses. Morning
fractals, summertime. Starry points.

A literal translation: our wee monsters advance

the hose, the wading pool, the sprinkler. The temporal similarity

of bees. This gentle rustling
of maple; sparkled leaves, a reach of trees impossible

to fathom.

2.

The boundary of   the sentence. Target birds,
an oriole or cackling jay.

Incomplete: the framework   of metaphor.
What

the poem can't help but resemble, a consequence
of choice and form, to

interrupt my patters, speech.

3.

The page is white but   is not blank.

Autobiography of green

1.

Each poem, at a particular time. A line of versets,
iambic feet. The children   , dither: compass

the backyard. Their summer playhouse, builds.

They wait, they wait.

Their perpendicular step.

2.

To speak of origins: the homestead,

iambic clay, the creek's

interminable motion. Striating fields, the fallow. Ice age
carving smith out of the ground.

Fluted points: such tenuous association. A drop
of glacial lakes.

3.

Precambrian shield. The first impulse, is
to sit. My   morning desk, at first light,

coffee. Too wide, to reach silence,

speechless reserve. If there   remain gods
to smite, to smother. How much might

that cost me? Where

my children patter, stray. Such danger, as far
as they might run.

4.

Parenting: helicopter, helicopter,

submarine. This glacial, rain. In order to write,

I write   this line

of thermal bridge.

Quarantine, in perpetua

1.

An astonishing kind of importance. To think, upon the page.

Any line that is composed can be reworked. Each word
in its proper place.

Rhythm and metre, neither of which are typing.

I mean this dialogue, quite literally. A kind of pleasure, often
    thought
as marginality.

In English, with context examples.

2.

One walks on silence, sound. One walks on eggshells. One walks

across an expanse   of Lego bricks, stuffed animals,
a stack

of colouring pages, books. Unlimited mirrors: the bearings
of our two children. Cheerios broadcast

the kitchen floor, and

each in their morning corners, tablets. They dress, escape
into the yard.

Two lines for *Pocket Lint*

The artisanal process of labour, as a poem
shedding leaves.

The Alta Vista Improvements

1.

To suffer detours: this through-line
of patchwork housing, outcrop. A craft

of optimism, ignorance. The internet equally
bears each alphabet.

Our 1950s dream-house,   capacious backyard,
deep. Trees peak, and ripple. An

undefinable mental space.

Lower sheets. They postcard. Feet fade from the offset.

2.

City ward named

for connecting tissue, thoroughfare. Did Thor invent lightning
or did lightning invent Thor?

Moments season, schedule

appreciations. The rumble of city bus, a firetruck.
Disambiguated,

suburban fractals. Bees forged hexagons, such
minimal density, and everything we construct

either collapse, or a half-life

of centuries. Poison the lake. It is possible
to exist without realizing.

3.

Oversimplified. Abbreviated streets. An architectural promise.

Every fourth yard, chlorinated pool water. David Hockney ripples.

4.

Sketch of hedges, fence-marks   , house
house, house. Is it possible to not be

a story of disappearance? A monstrous in-fill,
consuming former yard, disgorged. Obsolete.

Kevin Varrone: history is punctuated
by verticals.   Parallel marks

and geometric irregularities. Turns round. The mind
expects the grid.

What spring thaws reveal: nine months
of continuous construction. Chord

and chord and bell.

5.

This viewed obstruction   , frontier boundaries,
where once had been. A consternation

of paved sound. Greenspace, confidence. I put my house
in order. We know our histories,

edited. Washed out, hollow rhythms. Distractions
gap the paths.

Such grammar, loss. Mere words   arranged on paper.

6.

A dog day, silence: summer. Poem, gentrifies.
Poorly framed, and captured. Expand

the page; tear down
the yard, this

shoddy construction. By definition: you can still
hold your breath.

Burning the dead grass

1.

A farmer's springtime ritual: layers of controlled burn,
orange flames peeled black. Pressurized by winter snow,

this wild silken pasturage   grown brittle; to allow
fresh growth, injects

the lone, lit match.

These drifts   and banks
of unkempt tallgrass, clover, resting at the fence brow

, up and down the gravel boundaries
of concession seven. My youthful passage: accompanying

my father, as he attends

an authority of supervision: train of smoke, a furrow, one can see
for panoramic miles. Neighbouring farmers

who similarly announce: their rising, thin exhaust. The wake

of black crunch   , underneath my dusty runners.

2.

Once upon a time in North Stormont, Glengarry; the divisions
set, and imprecise. A carve of lineations

across assembly, immigration. Concession lines, the character arc

of geographic space. Aside traditional acreage set as pathways
connecting Kanien'kehá:ka, Ottawa foundations. Lands

116

I had to research. Monty Reid: No way to distinguish

what one has chosen to remember

from what one has chosen to forget. What these translations
can't yet identify, the unacknowledged breaks. Lineages

the settler descendants do not reference.

3.

My father's eightieth birthday   , he has been
    dead
for more than a year.

4.

For these forms to be original, they require self-awareness,
thought. Hard inertia:

Keats' dictum of ease, if a poem requires work. If even thought
requires work. I spend as much time extracting words

as I might introduce. A carved precision. The smoke lifts,
white and brown and black; subject to paternal shadow,

early 1980s, this Saturday morning

sparks a flutter. My father and his hired man
attending   shifts of air, and rain.

Monty Reid: It is not the first time   I have tried
to give up some words.

Four poems on receiving the Pfizer Covid-19 vaccine (second shot,

1.

At our local community centre, one neighbourhood over: a Pfizer
    chaser
following my original AstraZeneca. My cousin at the door,
    directing

foot traffic, unraveling

length upon length. Yellow-tape arrows. Our first
in-person chat in months.

The parking lot bullhorn, announcing appointments

in five minute intervals. Fifty-six days between shots,
the lowest

recommended allowance. That fine line
between the possible, recognizable only

as form. You made it   exactly, they told me.

2.

Slow, slow down. An ache, within the muscle. Low energy. Why
am I so, all of a sudden,

deflated? Birds or trees, might pause
in flight. Cool rain, cements. Can barely move,

can barely move. Fatigued. Two days
in a fog of exhaustion, catching up   on stacks of
    comics.

As far from sentimentality   as possible.

3.

My sister, my birth mother, uncle: refusals to vaccinate.
Neither vaccines   nor pandemics

care anything   for politics. A displacement,

and a glint of light. My sister posts
conspiracies to social media, refuses to discuss, conflates

disagreement with opposition, judgement. It isn't
out here, she says. Her local news says otherwise: more than

one hundred

and twenty cases in North Stormont. A low number,
but a number, still. All the cars on the highway,

all the birds in the parking lot,

are friends.

4.

Heart lingers   in the body. A love
divorced from logic. If every health protection agency,

every medical body in North America,

there is hardly betrayal   in wishing you safe.
Anxiety   , withers. I would rather be
     wrong

in every instance. Rosmarie Waldrop: This glint

of light   on the cut.

Autobiography

1.

Intimation, and the whole
of the poem. Ringo Starr: his early morning meander

in *A Hard Day's Night* (1964), a scene originated

as the young lad too hung over
from the night prior

to do much else. One knows the language,
and the frame of reference. Love and terror; the body

and our means. This long tidal reach, across
forty-five navigation locks. The possibility

of leaving everything intact

is overwhelming.

2.

Invasions, glance. Rhetorical, amid
the constant shift. Embanking floodplains,

a triptych of valley, gateway,
estuary. The Tower of Babel, and

the full weight

of cultural history. Some greyhounds
can sink

like a stone.

3.

Rarified: capturing the shadows
of a wordless art. Beatlemania. He walked the day's breath,

the glint of light on the cut. Britain's shoreline
of liquid history: this medial

muddy

watercourse. Ringo Starr, with each
dense step. Strolled solo, monochrome

and sepia, his perambulation

along the River Thames towpath,
the embankment in Kew, Surrey. The Neolithic page,

horizon. One of the very best
in London.

Summer, pandemic

1.

Reading Etel Adnan's *Seasons*, I perch in precooked car
and await our cat, attend this follow-up appointment

to his recent dental extraction. This body as a means

to dialogue, and his teeth held
in synaptic space. From this lone parking lot

in Ottawa's east end, veterinarian staff report his outbursts,
    frustrated

at their prodding. He is such
a mood.

2.

I read my book: a constant shift
of mourning, shallows. She mentions stiffness,

rain, and wind. Under sun's corrosive eye,

self-conscious breath, of breathing. Face-masked.
And yet, to say the truth: three

withering dandelion heads on the passenger side,
half an orange crayon on the floor mat.

A shadowed road. A crosswind.

3.

The hottest Vancouver on record. The hottest Ottawa
on record. The hottest Toronto

on record. The hottest Pakistan
on record. Our own details

have betrayed us. Adnan: Our civilization's
growth is cancerous.

4.

As we move through, seasons. Clouds, this
stagnant air. An asphalt

of reflected heat.

This is a time travel story: for sale, cat's
Elizabethan collar, newly worn. The painkillers

we administer, with the usual contusions.
At nine years old,

his age

is finally matched to mine. Old enough to undermine
the logic

of the pre-determined body.

5.

Confronts the table leg,
the chair leg, his

water bowl, and loses. This plastic cone
a rhetorical theatre

he can't conceive. A week's worth of
auto-generated

hang-dog expression.

6.

Four teeth removed, including, ironically enough,
his feline canines: costs enough

we could have purchased

another car. Our cat is now
a car. Small engine roars, and roars,

and hums.   I drive him finally home,

a threaded language for every future.

Sketchbook:

But these clouds, these fallen leaves, belong to History too,
Etel Adnan, *Seasons*

1.

Prince Edward County, summer: a temporal
desert.   Machine noise. Father-in-law,

a new garage. Rose attends
her virtual summer school morning; Aoife,

her language class. The German articulation
of numbers, pets. The self

in perpetual ease.

2.

Attend, the water's surface. Post-cataracts,
this the first summer I can fathom distance,

opposing shores. Divinations,
buoys, water fowl. Cars flow beyond

a patchwork of trees, banks. A long

descriptive passage. Panopticon

of meditations
flowing lakeside, differs. Docks.

3.

A bare sketch   , windows, gather. Sleek.
Wee monsters

abide, this borrowed pool. Carnivorous,
free fall. Aoife bounces off the board,

left hand in air, right forefinger, thumb

press closed her nostrils. Splash, an open
amplitude. It breaks   the tension.

4.

Binoculars might alter   cottage vistas.
Perpetually in motion. Land

for sale, house: waterfront property. This
urban encroachment. Set forth,

advancing homes, hotel,
all freshly stewed. Such Loyalist trace along the margins.

Airplane chatter. Where the

original habitants might very well   have gathered,
a whitewash

English sameness. Antiquity
holds no bounds but

memory.   Each winter
warms the bed.

5.

Aoife chirps German words for pencil, dog, cat. Christine
attends. This stitch of language tethers

air to ground, pool
and water's surface. Two workmen set

garage foundation. Orange shirts in midday light.
History bounds at high speed, slush. Glacial.

Composition

1.

I write in order to write. I write this, this,
that. One folds in sheets of paper, thus. The shape

these days have manufactured. There is no end, beyond
such personal residue.

2.

Boundless. Two replacement lower molars
I dare not ponder. Sedation, please. The bones

collapse. The finest jawbone that he's seen.

Rose and Aoife have eye appointments

1.

A confirmation of vision: four eyes
between them. Each test, projected. The speech

and image

of digital type. Deflated sounds,
as visible as air.

2.

On McLeod Street, named for a son
who lived a life of service. I settled, briefly, here,

and twice   across two decades. The children
are indifferent. Can we

go get McDonald's?

3.

A set   of leafy branches,
backdrop: office towers

cluster. To bear, Rose whistles

a simple tune.

4.

A former sign on Kilborn, stating
house number aside business name, "1285

Optometrists." The misread

will never not be funny.

5.

Their eyes are fine. Come back, he says,

in two years   , thereabouts.

Composition

1.

In the early stages of this writing, there
was simply no place

to put a period. I attempt to utilize
tension. My in-laws continue to believe

I should cut my hair. The tension
is manifest.

2.

Fourteen lines, with which to apply, opportune
or convey. The pace at which

one stakes, and states,

these complimentary emblems.
The trouble   with normal, or the language

of God: one of senses, rubble.

3.

All the years it took to write
that one sentence.

Ars Persona

1.

At the front of our yard, this elderly crabapple tree
in the neutral singular, the weight

of its branches, tearing a path to the ground. Leaning hard,
finally ripped through a silence

and shed like a palm. What we had thought
a good posture

of purpose, of musculature. Christine mourns, we
salvage crabapples, we ring the arborist

to assess the remains.

2.

A familial tumult. My mother's devilled eggs,
recreated, at best. My sister and her husband, home-made

roasting spit, the pig

a set of hours, days. A disassembly of get-togethers,
gatherings. In the company

of so much invention. Here, these feet
were ever feet, digesting

potluck dishes, stoneware, the scales
and procession

of seasonal interplay. All
on pandemic hold.

3.

To aim, with consistency. The insoluble present.

To fold in, with purpose. The yellow slick
of summer peaches, or how crabapples stain black

into pawprints, just there along driveway,
the sidewalk. In the company   of fibres,

an application of decades. The old growth

of septennial timber.   These days
develop wings. To make peace with the past

requires a perspective   that might not always

be possible.   In British Columbia, this
is the summer of wildfires. My sister, in her

unvaccinated car,

drives headlong into it.

The Garden

1.

Conversation: the shape   , and the duration.
An evening, left to stretch

past tenderness,   an August grip

of summer soil, tumblers. Kimberly and Alex, in
our socially-distant backyard. As Kimberly wrote: deep

as a ruffled pool.

2.

Tucked in, behind suburban brick, this metreage that occupies
such amplitude. Christine gardens,

a meritocracy of garlic, calendula, goldenrod,
    lavender
and lemongrass; a disposition   of tomatoes.

Her half-forgotten horseradish, leftover from last year, nearly
enough to separate

the skin of the earth like a tumor.

3.

In the children's corner garden, a pumpkin
appears, unexpectedly. What

they did not plant.

Tanya Lukin Linklater: A person enters and reads.

As in Nowhere, No-One

1.

Olympic-sized: the ocean's entirety, an
infinite weight.   You might scope out

four hundred metres, just shy

of a quarter-mile. Run, the sturdy arch. Such ancient history
of periphery, the continental slope. Our maple turn

and red. The anthem sings. Dawn hours move through water.
Strangers stand the podium, begun. A thought

that counts.

2.

Aside the racetrack, unshaded bleachers
remain fractioned. A garnering

of nesting fowl. Focus,

one might wager. Pundits: the   unvarnished thought.
     Silence
and the great merit of unspoken speech. The Nihilist

Spasm Band: I have nothing to say,
but I can say it very well.

3.

One might think   of turf-type grass,
of vertigo. High velocity bike-wheels clash

, clatter. A solitude
of salty wash.   Each sport

requires centre, muzzle. The smell of movement
into animal shapes, distorted hyphen

of this tannic wind. Priscila Uppal: If you cannot
locate me, to the millimetre. I would

confront these seasons, depth.

4.

On CBC Radio, Chuck Berry sings his brown eyed

handsome man. We are fresh

and singular beings. Don't think too hard. The news

is next.

Approximation

1.

The ragged edge of cloud formation. The gap
at the seam

of shadow   , gesture. Our cat,

his open mouth.   How long these days,
will soon swing short again. Too soon. An empathy

of substance. This fragrance
of approaching rain.

2.

As Mei-mei Berssenbrugge writes: What ignorance
can her description eliminate?

Some days, existing as a human is hard. Today
I am a bird.

3.

The sentence, gathers. These elements
gain weight. If the familiar path either

tightrope   , tether. Iambic woods.
A path, or where

the runoff, rain

has drained the topsoil. This narrow
puff of smoke.

From an essay on Jean Valentine and Emily Dickinson by Julie Carr

1.

Snow-blind, Sunday. This latent summer heat
that guides each phrase.

The whole air on the ground, another
wheelbarrow filled with topsoil. Damn,

the light thins fast. As crucial to notice
what further, dangled skills.

Myth, resembles. Comments and adornments,
trifecta terms of process. Whereas,

a successful writer 'rounds the nerves.

2.

As crucial as this writing. Oversimplifies:
preschooler has a cough. This goes on

for days. Such confident syntax: the pitter-patter
of iambic feet. In any case. The final lines

would serve to mention.

3.

Out of spiritual yearning, outrage. Levied
deeper questions. I wash one handprint

from the window. I wash one handprint
from the bathroom wall. I wash one handprint

from the fridge door handle. Five fingers,
slowly, slow. It might not matter.

4.

The poem imagines, imagines.

Awake, the measuring eye.

Heat wave

1.

It is so hot in Ottawa this week. "How hot
is it?"   Throw numbers around, like

heat wave index, and humidity. The timetable
of global sear. The limitations

of how we process meaning.

2.

The children lay downstairs in the cool, suburban
wasteland. Lego traps and Netflix. Can

we have a snack, please? Later. The poem
rises up an octave. They

relent, or I do.

To strive for greatness, and not knowing. Will
I ever write again.   I reread

a poem by Caroline Knox, her ghazal

on bone. It slowly   breaks the skin.

3.

A master of landscape, and architecture.
The arborist

trims and shreds the torn half
off our crabapple vista. Carved,

and boiled. A jar of newly minted. Crabapple jelly, left

in neighbours' hands: Wendy, to our immediate north,
and our latest, Brian, to the south;

the house

with the pool. He says, again, come over
anytime. Crabapple branches mulch

and disappear. Loose apples

bounce and stall across the bike lane,
firm and nearly ripe. By morning,

they'll evaporate. Street sweepers
compose their meditative pass; hard

and thoughtful, ease.

4.

How mathematics   is hard-wired
to never lie. Wave, this third; set forth,

we can go home again.

Come fly with me. Western Pacific, an island
sporting bone fragment

and a scrap of leather. Nikumaroro, in
the Phoenix Islands. Amelia Earhart,

so they say,

might finally land.

Reading Kaveh Akbar's *Pilgrim Bell* by our new inflatable pool

1.

This lyric footnote   to our two wee girls. Across
suburban stillness, a second

pandemic summer. Inflate, this choral beast. To lifeguard,
catch their chaos: now

they've gathered swimsuits, sunscreen, neon sun hats; towels
discarded, strewn across the lawn. The garden hose

enables water levels, slow. The fallow ether,
heat. Compels.

Kaveh Akbar: God's word is a melody,
and melody requires repetition.

2.

I largely believe in neither God nor absolutes. My personal blend
of atheist, and agnostic. I am not certain

what I don't believe. Tommy Pico: Nations

are always outlived by their cities. So too
of deities, to faithful; a routine   erosion

of both memory

and the body. Today, the children
laugh at splashing, tumbles. Thick, this compilation: blue

of summer sky. The air

is static   , stock-still.

3.

The difficulty   of solitude. Ongoing months
of household isolation. Either child, upset at any suggestion

of separation. An outdoor day-camp. Aoife
cries at drop-off, every morning

for the full week.   Our daughters
are home, are always home. And we, too.

As quick   as a half-thought. A subtweet
takes time. Kaveh Akbar: God's word

is a melody, and melody requires repetition.

4.

The last time I saw my father he was dead. I expect, for him,
that little has changed. His youngest grandchildren

apply wet, dirty footprints

across our kitchen floor, en route
to main floor bathroom. I have to go, they yell. The digital display

on my cellphone, sluggish. A second pair

of towels replace
what they've already abandoned.

5.

Polyvinyl chloride: inflatable stripes of white and deep blue,
held to ground, our personal echo

of the ozone ceiling. It swells

such temperate, watery mass. I turn the page, and then
another. The shade of absolute integrity,

an afternoon of poems. A sweltering of what
the week brings.   Uncomfortable

with otherwise allowing our ladies solo
in this foot or so

of grassy, leafy soup.

6.

The children break for snacks. Sun hats: discarded splash
of neon texture

on uneven green. In two week's time,

we commit my father's ashes. There,
just upon my mother. Such a long death, sixteen months

of mourning, incomplete; since that first dawn
he wouldn't wake. Kaveh Akbar: God's word

is a melody,

and melody requires repetition.

7.

As writing prompt, Sawako Nakayasu says to select
an object or concept. Write a poem. Write another. *Write poems*

in this manner

for as long as you can. The children two days prodding
for the pool and ninety minutes filling it, less

than an hour

before back in the house.

Composition

1.

This week's apoplectic mood. It quickens, curls.
A poem's lament   , darkens. I was exactly

today years old   before I learned that random fact

I hadn't known. Is this important? A chorus
of media and interactive platforms

bestowing false and equal weight

to a new Marvel Cinematic Universe film trailer, and the onset
of Taliban rule in Afghanistan.

How language holds   each fissure. How
the clouds part.

This notebook fragment: the bare minimum.

2.

The children breakfast   at kitchen peninsula.
A single butter knife sprouts from open Nutella jar, loose scraps

of pre-sliced brown. A paired barrage
of tablet noise a mass   they somehow distinguish

between oatmeal spoons. Once done, they grab devices,
surrender bowls,

and barrel down the hall, to dress. It is someone's turn

to feed the cat.

3.

The etymology   of bread, and the history
of the mechanical slicing process.

Introduced in 1928, when American actress Betty White
was six years old. Sliced bread,   the greatest thing

since Betty White.

Associations, gather.   This
might be a window, window, door. A leaf buckles,

breaks   , makes landfall. Leans in,

underneath the grass. As children emerge
from backyard, blades of breadcrumb grass

release from shoes to carpet,
hardwood.

4.

I do not struggle with the poem, but with
my own attentions.

Valzhyna Mort: Sometimes our words   can cut meat.

The back of fire, curved. From one language

to another. I slip out, step away. The outdoor view,
so Alta Vista smooth. Cars trundle, bus.

And for a spell,   all else is quiet.

Pastoral

1.

Wildfires. The midday sun.   Red-orange light
tones rust. Sky a smokey blend of bronze

and umber. Unable to locate   the moon. The
    seas

have bleached. Have all run dry.

2.

Canadian Lakes, Michigan. Akin to "French Doors," a lake
in the Canadian style. Named

for the ways in which

it reminded the founder of Canadian landscapes. This
is an echo, and echoes

ripple. In 1963, Donald Bollman had a vision,
and that vision was exclusive.

3.

Via Twitter, Chen Chen offers up the moon, and the "mare
    humorum,"
his favourite of these impact basins: craters

mistaken by the early astronomers
for lunar seas. The sea

of moisture, where it lay, and had been, for some

three-point-nine billion years. The dissolution
of a misread word. Oh,

to plant a garden.

4.

If I could sow a seed of moon. If I could plant it
in that auburn glow. This august body:

green corn, sturgeon, grain
or red.   To see above

such intermittent light. Compact
and held, the distance   of the lunar surface.

5.

You poets. Why can't you leave the moon
alone.   You monsters.

Autobiography

1.

The argument of which month may indeed
be cruellest. On the biographical level, it breaks

us apart. I keep circling this pond   like a fish.

2.

Rosmarie Waldrop: everything   inside everything.

The skin you can't restore   , an epiphany
across metaphor. The social media glint

in the light   of the cut. What the calendar
is wishing

to tell you. All   the takes are bad.

3.

I felt   some kind of collision,
and the whole building   shook.

If it keeps on rainin', the levee's

gonna break. Hurricane Ida: the alternate logic
of circumstance.

A whole life   writing, reduced
to a sentence or two.   A hard rain.

4.

I can't   ; the social media discourse

burns the skin, the surfaces
across ionosphere. Why can't you just,

: an exposition   of impossible furor.

5.

To compose   in the third person,
second. One writes

not a silence, but still. To respond
to the noise. This particular order.

John Newlove: the arrangement   is all.

6.

How poetry makes nothing
happen. The inflection and stress

on that final word.

Four poems for *Mary: A Journal of New Writing*

1.

Ranchero philosophies, the translation
of the sort of art

that colonialism requires. The Bay Miwok, Saklan. Her breath
catches fire. A book of questions

one could barely contemplate

as literature. In every poem,
to reinvent the line.

2.

Norma Cole: when

does the past
begin?

At Canyon Road, a failed bridge.

3.

This order of preachers, ranchers,

Christian brothers. To articulate between, the sound
and analog silence. No matter how strenuous,

coined; with reckless freedom, heart, the possibility

of collective salvation. And to know how much
the bounds of which

are endless.

4.

A door closing, creaks. That's how
my poem ends.

Rose finally gets a fish

1.

Her months of drawings, pressure   ; reminders
to our whispered ears, to

plastering the fridge with several clones

of her single magnet-held artwork: "fish," she writes, above
each sketch of same, "I want one." I, for one,

hesitate to introduce a new character

into this household menagerie, with the increased risk
of cancelling the whole business. Richie's brother Chuck

from *Happy Days*' first season, or to simply

jump the shark.

2.

She wants a fish.   Demands: a pet of her own,
to share with younger sister,

since I refuse to entertain a dog   ; our cat
would tarnish, and my difficulty with lack

of unaccompanied urban territory. A dog

requires an excess   unavailable. I originated
from a farm   , after all, where dogs

possess the amplitude
to roam.   Preferring, also, not

a defecated yard. Rose   wants a fish, she
wants a fish, she wants a fish. In case

the message was unclear. She offers
promises of pet care and routine,

hoping someone will believe her.

3.

Bellwether, prep; to establish and assemble her aquarium

before any fish might land. Rose plucks

a castle, mermaid   , small plastic greenery; harvests
two small bags of coloured gravel. Her bearing, shifts,

she vibrates, crosswise; strums   PetSmart
    shelves.
Each step

a stop, a break   in linearity. She laughs,

ahead of her own debate. With fresh tank sidelining
her seasonal e-learning retreat

of former dining room, she holds: the soon-keeper

of the sacred fish.

4.

This biological   filter media. Her fishless
ten-gallon vessel, which will be,

soon enough. How water catches sound
in motion, motion. Apparently boundless. This approximation

of a single misstep, stanza,

verset, word. Once home, and set   , she stares, across

this dimpled glow   of light-emitting diode
into oxygenating water.

Yesterday, not my photo

1.

This tornado's funnel kiss along the waters of Lake Huron.

Port Albert beach: a foreign language might be stripped

of borders, nothingness. The air thins, tinny. The scent

of low pressure vacuum. The hairs along each arm.

2.

When Amy and Andrew visited, he and I gathered

our combined small children—two

toddlers, two infants—for a playground jaunt. I caught

the shift in the air and said, we have to go. We held

our boundaries. This onslaught of rain. We barely made

the threshold   of the front door.

3.

Environmental. I wish to make my questions

known, from lifted references. My beloved clash.

I found this image on the internet, I no longer

remember where. But it makes my point.

Displacement: where the rain meets silence,

where the word meets open space. The calm

converts to lawn.

My father rode in a helicopter

1.

Before his Amyotrophic Lateral Sclerosis diagnosis, my father
traversed a stretch of Eastern Ontario

in an air ambulance emergency helicopter. Unable
to properly breathe,

before they discovered   his lungs become too
    weak

to discharge carbon dioxide. The syntax
of exhalation: this orange helicopter, arriving

somewhere at the homestead   to transport
    him
the hour's drive

to the Ottawa General Hospital. As the crow flies,
a distance only he has travelled. Whatever else

I might have garnered,
that would have been worth seeing. Did it land

in an adjacent field? The driveway? Did it make
a big noise? Did it

frighten my father's dog?

Nearly eight unbroken decades on singular property, feet firm

on the ground, my father: his premier
helicopter jaunt. Was he able   to enjoy it?

2.

At fifty-one, I have outlived Paul Celan, Jack Spicer, Frank O'Hara,
and will never be, thankfully,

a member of the twenty-seven club. At nearly eighty, my father

outlasted most of his parents' generation, some by more
than twenty years,

surviving cancer surgery and a triple-bypass, knowing

either heart or cancer discharged the entire assembly
of his immediate relations. Fifty-one and adopted, both

of my birth parents

are still of this world: at times, one appreciates the articulation
of alternate genes.

3.

As my birth mother offers: I've much

from her matrilineal path: Whitteker hair
and Whitteker eyes. Early cataracts. A social energy. To introduce

this list

of previously unknown genealogical details

I've yet   to fully incorporate. Fragments formed
of words, alone. To fractal into parts once mine,

a complex web of interconnected selves.

4.

Christine suggests I misunderstood: my father gasped,
my sister delivered by car   to their local ER, a
    helicopter

not at homestead, but instead, from their
small regional hospital. As the crow flies. Hardly

a period   of reflection. Or a comma. So easily
worn, worn out. He could   not breathe.

5.

Was time   not different, then? What rare, unwieldly
    crow
might soar in one sustained direction. An absence

that spreads through the bones.

Charles Dickens, *Oliver Twist* (1838): *We cut over the fields*
at the back with him between us – straight

as the crow flies – through hedge and ditch. And yet, that hardly
sounds direct.   Clouds drift, clouds drift and
    spill,

and still spill, light.

6.

My father,   his once-charcoal tussle, crow-black,

eroded over time to silver   grey   to
    white; reduced
to ash. Where my sister set him, there, in the soil,

just by our mother. I'm sure she complained. The headstone
already his adjacent name. In the end   , it was where

he needed to be.

Who I am today

1.

A preternatural occurrence: a poem drops from the sky
like a bird

or a spider. How to respond to it. This juxtaposition
of commonality. A smell

to return one   to childhood.

2.

Such philosophical stance. This tendency away

from analogy. Notes, as one
takes an axe. All the trees

in the forest.

3.

Whether the deepest rivers are, in fact. These waterways
bone-dry. This is not a river. How many years

have we always been home. The silence, formed

at the end of each line.

Rose collects a second fish, to replace the first one

1.

Eighteen hours   beyond introducing "Princess"
to aerated, tested ten gallon mere   , she lay

on blue-pebbled bed. Our original purchase,
she remained, unmoored   , unmoved,

until we salvaged her body. Sunk
to the boards

like a stone. Our young ladies announced: the fish
is dead! Perhaps   she is but asleep, we

countered, worried
as to their reactions. Reader: she was never asleep.

2.

The fish   is dead, and it's
so lonely

by a brightly-coloured resin castle   , mermaid,
limb. Rose crafts a portrait, profile

of her fish, an X across
the single, visible eye.

But one light   brighter
than the other. In the centre, Princess' former

roommate snails   draw circles in their pleats.

3.

The fish we have is not   the one we leave behind.

A second visit, return and acquisition. "Sparkle," added
after consultation, testing,

re-testing. *Yours is the finest water*

I've seen in months, the staff claimed, from his corner
of the PetSmart territory. How what is said differently

is difference enough. And yet,
this new fish   dead, a second

body in a step of days. Twenty-four hours later.

It is so lonely   on a limb.

4.

We pause, refresh. Christine admits: I don't wish to explain death
a third time.   What else to add? The explanation

no different. This is death, and death
a constant. There is nothing further

to articulate. Both fish

are dead. I head back in, receipt in-hand, once more
attempting resolution, answers. Reimbursement. The snails

contain such fully-clothed   intelligence. They leave
such marks.

5.

The fragmentation   of this liquid hope.

Autobiography

1.

An archaeology   of human contact. The map
has been scaled

or whittled down. A jumpy sentence. I am too loud

on the outdoor, restaurant patio. Distanced,
marked and traced.

2.

If what we thought at the beginning   had anything
to do with this, with now. Stephen scans

a barcode, surfaces the menu. If prepositions
contain substantive, concussive force. If only.

3.

I fear   for that which I currently lack.
The wallpaper

of our former comforts, selves.
Beneath your mask,

I have forgotten the look   of your face.

Four poems for Douglas Barbour
(1940–2021)

1.

When words   slip, clear. The simplicity
of affirmation. Breath:

    , a heady mixture of *ashy*

stubble such fire leaves we might discover

, and a reference to text. This bungalow
in Belgravia. His elastic precision   of shelves.

2.

Mid-gasp, short-winded   , spent. Beneath

the bright blue, as if
                the whole place held its breath.

His ghazals   of abounding respirations.

How form, once held, is less discursive. Responding to,
responding to, responding to. Each phrase is carved,

and caved, streamlined. For eternity,

as might have been.

3.

The plains-parkland divide. Such runoff: old kindred,

fathomless: *that heart knelt   all offended / pardon.*
As a tourist, to only remember   knowing. But

he never was. Writing west, and west
through hearth's Colorado Spruce and Balsam Poplar,

        surround. *Snowdeaf*: core

of simple dark. The North Saskatchewan River.
Entries   of a single journey.

Legion: this alphabet   of implicit action.

4.

From his origins in Winnipeg to a life lived   , well and deep,
in Edmonton, a story   for a Saskatchewan night. As
    high

as a highway. Outstretched. This fragmentation, accrued

amid borders of genre   , the open door. To play
an instrument you love,

        I know the song well; and repair

to his complex forest of poetics. The car, never idles.
Turns off the ignition.

        This *soft inhalation of air.*

        That *easy breath easing out.*

Four poems for Peter Van Toorn
(1944–2021)

1.

Famously abrasive,   O, old rumpled legend, this

retired poet, contained and stationed past the Seigneury of
    Rigaud,
in Valois, a village within the village

of Pointe-Claire   where, as they say, nothing

ever happens. Baudelaire on the hill, the mountain tea
of cylindrical stone windmills   , the limestone quarry

below the Beaconsfield Golf Course.

Within his smoke-glazed kitchen walls;   tobacco-stained,
the sharp abrasions

of his voice   a thing you can hear

for kilometres, years. Or the underbody   of cars.

2.

Hail Mary, encased in stone,   bound up

in stark, depleted pages; no-one singing Mass. The wind at his
    back,

into his throat, or where the soul lay. Roll-your-own, his
    burnished

fingertips might parse out   scrapbook lines,
    to carve

your breath away.   His, a storm that never fully

lost its teeth   in the ethical mud. Chaotic fall,
such divinity he understood, as deep   and thick

as Vermeer: introducing light and heavy dark into
this cultured monochrome, this landscape

of Quebecoise snow,

: long-loined   and sublunary curved.

3.

This peerage   of wind, where

there's hardly air. He'd smoked it out. Of fire, water, earth;
of stone. A body of poems homespun, forged

in iron, clay, half-whispered prayer. Of steel. Combustion,

, this tempest fit for striking, swinging. Through gravel scratch,
he plucked flame from the matchbook flash,

his one true, lyric offering.

4.

O, this damned climate   of cardboard, lumber lads
who sweat and know not why; of measured, rakish swings

and corresponding slaps, he sang
until his voice broke. Steerage,   grisly, threadbare

bees and sterling chorus. What you take from this shaved

and single stone   , steeped fresh,

this life-long book.   An orbit of clouds, determined
        countenance
of cannabis fog. Wrung out,   seismic, sudden. Where

and when the wind wins, finally. Where it marked the smell,
and coaxed it into morning.

Autobiography of blue

1.

The limits of this lack   of definition: first snows,
the powdered framework that erodes

often contrary   to what remains. Two-pronged. A line
        repeats,
evaporated. Warm weather: the weaponization

of arrangement.

2.

It snows   , but does not stay. Around these parts

, whole generations of trick-or-treaters   securing hand-
        picked costumes
under layered, thermal strata: sweaters, jackets, scarves

and snowpants. Only   masks betray. *And
what are you supposed to be? A Dracula?* Two years back:

carting jogging stroller and our two wee,   costumed monsters: a
        bearing,
saturated, beneath unseasonal deluge

of cold, October rainfall.   Their pillowcases
stuffed to overflow.

Today's patterning is seasonal, delayed:

                within the bounds of composition. Sun's
pretentious rays. A patterning of dusty cloud.

3.

It remains too warm today

for supersaturated air   , this atmospheric vapour
of water droplets

to crystallize or shape. As form requires: each flake that nucleates
around

a dust particle. Ashes to powder, our bodies fall
into the shape of snow.

4.

The season weathers, wears. An air of mystery: should we
turn up the heat? Secure the garden from frost? Christine: I
    opened

the bedroom window last night

for ventilation. Our two children, barefoot, in leaf-marbled yard.

To breach this memory   even
as it forms. A splinter, snowflake; lodged.   The sun

is hollow   : an embroidered sequence
or a key

into this language.

5.

Imagine: I walk out the door directly into   airborne sea
of snowflakes.   If only.

Six anti-ghazals for Phyllis Webb
(1927–2021)

1.

The distance   houses. Ninety-four years,
deliberating *Ideas*, backstage with Leonard,

or crafting failure, enough
until it, too, could sing.   Hermetic sounds.

Artifacts of blessings, common good.

The echo reflects   across the imprint

of such ancient curve. A bowl, perhaps. This stone
upon the question.

To revise on paper and endlessly   think.

2.

No writer   an island. A stone's throw
seeking tether,   shorelines. On Salt Spring,

where she lay   books aside.

A correspondence   : the small hand
of an outpost. Fierce, and fiery. A copy of her essays,

signed. A wedding present. The closing pages

held, and scattered. Fell ,   against this
floating detour.

3.

The argument of moments   , memorials.
Monuments. John Newlove, also. Cross-legged

in a room. The memo   of an artifact. Naked.
To highlight care, and gentleness. Two ladybirds, spin.

This texture of blossoms. Sundeck. A space of intimacy,
to land on spitting dust. Ascribe the mainland. Long shadow, gulf.

The paintbrush   or the shutter.

Capacity   of the single page.
Where you have left   your mark.

4.

My mentors are dying. Friends. Douglas Barbour, Joe Blades,
David Donnell. Incomparable speech.

Michael Dennis. Bless your cotton socks.

Cold   , this curse of weather. Green island grass.
A footpath, there, approaching Royal Canadian Legion Branch 92.

Illumination, illumination. More than I have. More
than I might comprehend.

A cobweb, across   the field of the sayable,
towards the white frame.

5.

Gerard Manley Hopkins: "I am happy, so happy." Last words,
set against a silence. Certified, crafted. Coiled.   As
        careful

as a phrase. Iambic pleasure. Brief candle, pen. Lone typescript.
Salt Spring Garbage Services   : what saturated air

; this modest shed of mildewed paperbacks.

Her hand-scrawled autograph   decorating discards.
Island restoration, salvage   , refreshed

and undiminished. Books, perpetual   ;
        released
into the undercurrent.

6.

Heidegger, Heidegger. The wood   still split.
Her brother's gift of scotch. The ferry, lace

and thread. An ebb. An alphabet

of broken skin. Meniscus. This daylight spread
like plush. We watch this morning passenger, port

into the unfamiliar. Alongside.   We watch
it occupy both absence,

space. This   peacock blue.
This crest and curl. We chase the furrows.

Rose finally gets a third fish,

1.

Two weeks beyond original purchase
and assembly of ten-gallon tank and fish regalia,

we appeal a different store, a different treatment plan, to seek out
alternate advice. Two fish dead across three days,

and how far my daughter's grief

might fall. A slate of unknown causes, and how
to best inquest the possibilities   of poor water quality,
    pre-

existing illness
or aquatic stress upon their wee fish hearts. Our two snails,
    abide.

2.

As they say, third time's   the charm:
to draw this thin black line, a gallows map; Rose's artwork

of her two lost pets, profile's single eye a hand-drawn X. All things
made out of nothing, something; a space forced

into mirror, and the physical fact   of language.
She wants   a fish: how far we've come, committed

to this depth of waterlogged absence. Two uncomplicated snails,
and the tank set up now temporarily   theirs, alone.

3.

The sheets of blank paper Rose pilfers
from my writing desk, her school-stash array of markers

through which she views   the heavens. The fish
in the tank is air, the fish in the tank

is earth, the gravel   in the tank a vital function.

4.

Rose and Christine dock at Big Al's Ottawa East; how present
a shipwreck   , into sentences. The way a word

can puncture, drill. Asphyxiate. Here, we listen

for familiar words: Rose plucks a new, replacement fish,
now what to name it. Christine suggests   "Sapphire,"

but Rose lands "Blacktooth,"   laughs
her wild turbulence. Long backward loop, towards

imagination. She meets the challenge of water
with water; there is

no fire. She boils, burns. Unrestricted by grammar.

5.

A flutter   on the water's surface. This hymn
to pet ownership: synchronal first attempt,   this third.

Once home,

this active male, pealed and petaled blue-black, and his slow
     acclimation
to the water's temperature. He floats

within transparent pouch   that bobs and hovers along

the meridian. Contained, serenely: swirls. His blind, incessant
     impulse
without knowledge. Let algae, creep. Arise: this fish

will live.

Acknowledgements:

Versions and variations of these pieces have appeared in print and/ or online via *Allium, A Journal of Poetry & Prose* (Chicago IL), *The Babel Tower Notice Board* (Glasgow, Scotland), *Balestra Magazine* (St. Catharines ON), *Buffalopluseight* (Buffalo NY), *Carousel* (Guelph ON), *Columba: online poetry quarterly* (Montreal QC), *Court Green* (Chicago IL), *CV2* (Winnipeg MB), *filling Station* (Calgary AB), *flo. Literary Magazine* (Ottawa ON), *Hamilton Arts & Letters* (Hamilton ON), *Miramichi Reader* (Miramichi NB), *Moist Poetry Journal* (US), *Mouse Eggs* (Montreal QC), *New Note Poetry* (Charlotte NC), *Pamenar Online Journal* (London, England), *Prairie Fire* (Winnipeg MB), *SAGINAW* (Beijing, China), *talking about strawberries all of the time* (Toronto ON), *Train: a poetry journal* (Toronto ON), *Vallum magazine* (Montreal QC) and *Watch Your Head* (Toronto ON), and broadcast on Nathanael G. Moore's *honorarium: the podcast* (Fredericton NB) and Alexandro Botelho's *Writings on the Wall* (www.youtube.com/c/ diversetv1). David Miller was good enough to produce the poem "Autobiography of green" as a leaflet (print and online) through his Kater Murr's Press (Dorset, England) in June 2021. Poems also appeared in the chapbook anthology *showing up: michael dennis: remembered in art and poetry*, ed. Stuart Ross (Cobourg ON: Proper Tales Press, September 19, 2021), and as the chapbooks *Autobiography* (Ottawa ON: above/ground press, 2022), *Poems for a return to the world* (London ON: Rose Garden Press, 2022), *The Alta Vista Improvements* (Ottawa ON: above/ground press, 2023) and *the sentence of the book* (Philadelphia PA: Ethel Zine, 2025). My thanks to all editors and publishers involved.

The "Autobiography" poems are for and after David O'Meara and John Newlove (1938-2003), originally prompted through a recollected 2019 conversation with O'Meara (at one of our VERSeFest meetings), referencing his own individual clusters of equally-named lyrics (his pieces in this vein were retitled by the time they made to book form via Coach House, his 2021 collection, *Masses on Radar*). The poem "Coordinates" was prompted by an equally-named poem by Caroline Knox, from her *Quaker Guns* (Wave Books, 2008). "The Alta Vista Improvements" riffs off phrases and lines from Philadelphia poet Kevin Varrone's *the philadelphia improvements* (ugly duckling presse, 2010) and *g-point almanac: passyunk lost* (ugly duckling presse, 2010), and the poem was first composed on my neighbour's deck, as our young ladies swam in their pool; thanks much to Brian Torgunrud for the Covid-era invitation, and the space. The poem "Burning the dead grass" folds in a line or two of Monty Reid's poem "Burning the Back Issues," lifted from his *flat side* (Red Deer Press, 1998). "Ars Persona," "The Garden" and "As in Nowhere, No-One" are responses to equally-titled poems by Kimberly Quiogue Andrews, from her debut collection, *A Brief History of Fruit* (University of Akron Press, 2020), and are dedicated to her and Alex, and their summer 2021 relocation to Ottawa. The italicized lines from "Four poems for Douglas Barbour" are lifted, seemingly at random, from either his *Story for Saskatchewan Night* (Red Deer College Press, 1990) or *Breath Takes* (Wolsak and Wynn, 2001).

Addendum: Rose's third fish, Blacktooth, died some seven months after initial purchase, following a brief illness. He will be missed. There was a fourth fish, and a fourth poem, but we shall save that for the next collection, "Autobiography."

Deep and ongoing thanks to Aritha van Herk for her larger structural suggestions, and to Helen Hajnoczky, for her clear eye, and delicate edits.

This collection sits in a straight line from *the book of smaller* (University of Calgary Press, 2022). Soundtrack: Sigur Rós, Beach House, Brian Eno.

This book is for my father
        and for Rosmarie Waldrop

    "It seems I have always been preoccupied with the sentence."

        Rosmarie Waldrop, "Rosmarie Waldrop in
        Conversation with Ben Lerner,"
        *Rosmarie and Keith Waldrop, Keeping / the
        window open: Interviews, statements, alarms,
        excursions*, ed. Ben Lerner. Seattle WA/New York
        NY: Wave Books, 2019

January 2019 – November 2021
2423 Alta Vista Drive, Ottawa

Photo Credit: rob mclennan, TELUS Spark Science Centre, Calgary, Alberta

ROB MCLENNAN is a writer, editor, publisher, critic, and the author of nearly fifty titles. His work has won the John Newlove Poetry Award and the Council for the Arts in Ottawa Mid-Career Award, and was longlisted twice for the CBC Poetry Prize. He lives in Ottawa, where he is home full-time with the two wee girls he shares with Christine McNair.

BRAVE & BRILLIANT SERIES

SERIES EDITOR: Aritha van Herk, Professor, English, University of Calgary
ISSN 2371-7238 (PRINT) ISSN 2371-7246 (ONLINE)

No. 1 · *The Book of Sensations* | Sheri-D Wilson

No. 2 · *Throwing the Diamond Hitch* | Emily Ursuliak

No. 3 · *Fail Safe* | Nikki Sheppy

No. 4 · *Quarry* | Tanis Franco

No. 5 · *Visible Cities* | Kathleen Wall and Veronica Geminder

No. 6 · *The Comedian* | Clem Martini

No. 7 · *The High Line Scavenger Hunt* | Lucas Crawford

No. 8 · *Exhibit* | Paul Zits

No. 9 · *Pugg's Portmanteau* | D. M. Bryan

No. 10 · *Dendrite Balconies* | Sean Braune

No. 11 · *The Red Chesterfield* | Wayne Arthurson

No. 12 · *Air Salt* | Ian Kinney

No. 13 · *Legislating Love* | Play by Natalie Meisner, with Director's Notes by Jason Mehmel, and Essays by Kevin Allen and Tereasa Maillie

No. 14 · *The Manhattan Project* | Ken Hunt

No. 15 · *Long Division* | Gil McElroy

No. 16 · *Disappearing in Reverse* | Allie McFarland

No. 17 · *Phillis* | Alison Clarke

No. 18 · *DR SAD* | David Bateman

No. 19 · *Unlocking* | Amy LeBlanc

No. 20 · *Spectral Living* | Andrea King

No. 21 · *Happy Sands* | Barb Howard

No. 22 · *In Singing, He Composed a Song* | Jeremy Stewart

No. 23 · *I Wish I Could be Peter Falk* | Paul Zits

No. 24 · *A Kid Called Chatter* | Chris Kelly

No. 25 · *the book of smaller* | rob mclennan

No. 26 · *An Orchid Astronomy* | Tasnuva Hayden

No. 27 · *Not the Apocalypse I Was Hoping For* | Leslie Greentree

No. 28 · *Refugia* | Patrick Horner

No. 29 · *Five Stalks of Grain* | Adrian Lysenko, Illustrated by Ivanka Theodosia Galadza

No. 30 · *body works* | dennis cooley

No. 31 · *East Grand Lake* | Tim Ryan

No. 32 · *Muster Points* | Lucas Crawford

No. 33 · *Flicker* | Lori Hahnel

No. 34 · *Flight Risk* | A Play by Meg Braem, with Essays by William John Pratt and by David B. Hogan and Philip D. St. John, and Director's Notes by Samantha MacDonald

No. 35 · *The Signs of No* | Judith Pond

No. 36 · *Limited Verse* | David Martin

No. 37 · *We Are Already Ghosts* | Kit Dobson

No. 38 · *Invisible Lives* | Cristalle Smith

No. 39 · *Recombinant Theory* | Joel Katelnikoff

No. 40 · *The Loom* | Andy Weaver

No. 41 · *Bonememory* | Anna Veprinska

No. 42 · *Love and War Western Style* | Rose Scollard

No. 43 · *Rag Pickers* | Blaine Newton

No. 44 · *What is Broken Binds Us* | Lorne Daniel

No. 45 · *the book of sentences* | rob mclennan

www.ingramcontent.com/pod-product-compliance
Lightning Source LLC
Chambersburg PA
CBHW051210090426
42740CB00022B/3456